THE POLITE DINOSAUR

By
Darshna Morzaria
Sanjay Morzaria

AuthorHouse™ UK
1663 Liberty Drive
Bloomington, IN 47403 USA
www.authorhouse.co.uk
Phone: 0800 047 8203 (Domestic TFN)
+44 1908 723714 (International)

Published by AuthorHouse 06/28/2019

ISBN: 978-1-5462-9729-1 (sc)
ISBN: 978-1-5462-9728-4 (e)

Print information available on the last page.

This book is printed on acid-free paper.

authorHOUSE®

Dedication

This book is dedicated to our daughter Nupur
(who's also happens to be our best friend).

To us, Nupur will always be our little dinosaur -
dominant and the biggest positive change in our lives.
Also hugely charismatic.

In return, still fail to understand how we are Nupur's
cashpoint machine dispensing endless cash on demand;
or
her MasterChef cooking her favourite meals on demand;
or
her 24/7 chauffeur.

Still, our little dinosaur is irreplaceable.

Foreword

"Wonderful use of rhyme to deliver the golden rules that are the constructive boundaries for all young children.

This book is about what children should do and not what they can't do. It's about activity, fun, safety, freedom, wellbeing, care and friendship - being active and the pleasure of being alive outside."

Tracy Seed

Early Years Consultant
tracyseed.com

About Tracy

For over 30 years, Tracey has helped individuals, families, schools and enterprises, from across the world, adopt mindsets and practical skills for partnership and collaboration in the art of relating.

About the authors

Darshna & Sanjay runs a unique and special Early Years nursery, from their own home. Their nursery is a home and workplace combined; warm and welcoming yet well-equipped, family-centred yet fully compliant with safety standards.

Children come to them at the very beginning of their learning journey, so they make their development their number one priority right from the start. They follow the Department of Education's Early Years Foundation Stage guidelines to provide each child with a comprehensive pre-school education. Children take part in a range of well-thought out, educational, interactive and inspiring activities on a daily basis.

On top of this, they lay the foundations for good citizenship and community-centered living. To help them do this, they employ only the most experienced, passionate and highly qualified staff.

The nursery puts each child at the heart of their family.

Ofsted rated as "Outstanding" in September 2018. In 2018 & 2019, they achieved a Silver in the internationally-renowned RoSPA Health and Safety Awards. In 2016, the nursery was shortlisted as a finalist in the coveted Nursery World Awards. This is the third published children's book following "The Big Yummy Treasure Chest" & "The Giraffe in the Garden".

LittleDarling.co.uk

 @LittleDarlingHa   Facebook.com/LittleDarlingHarrow   ▶ YouTube.com/c/LittleDarlingUK

Little Sammy got many things right,
But the boy just wasn't very polite!

His parents despaired of the way he behaved,
For a kind, friendly child, was something they craved.

He snatched and he shouted, he gulped down his food,
To the other poor kids, he was spiteful and rude.

His Mum called Sammy's nursery for a chat,
"Sammy isn't polite! Can you help out with that?"

Darshna, the manager smiled as she said,
"He's just got some funny ideas in his head."

"But he is so naughty", his poor mother chided.
"He's a good boy", said Darshna, "the child is just misguided."

"I think I can fix this with something I'll borrow,
Just make sure he comes to the nursery tomorrow."

When Sammy attended nursery the very next day,
For once the boy had nothing to say.

For standing so large at the nursery door,
Was a huge green scaly DINOSAUR.

"I'm Nupurasaurus", the dinosaur said.
"And I've come here to talk some sense into your head!"

"Apologies Sammy if I gave you a fright,
I'm just here to teach you how to be polite."

Sammy, in awe of this ginormous creature,
Could only agree with his new nursery teacher.

Five golden rules Nupurasaurus would cover,
To the great delight of his father and mother.

Be Helpful.

If someone's got into a muddle,
do things to help them get out of trouble.
And when someone struggles, ask what you can do.
I'm sure they'd do the same for you.

Sharing and Caring.

If you have too much stuff,
there may well be others who don't have enough.
Think about others throughout the day.
Be caring and kind, it's the nursery way!

Take Turns.

Don't keep to yourself all the best books and toys,
Share with the other girls and boys.
There's plenty of things to go round it is true,
Some for me and some for you.

Be Friendly.

Every helper is a friend in disguise,
So smile and be friendly, it really is wise.
It's never too late to start being kind,
You can do it Sammy, just press rewind!

Always try Hard.
Our final rule.
Just do your best and life will take care of all the rest.
Try your hardest every day and things will start to go your way.

Sammy followed Nupurasaurus round all day,
Learning to act in the nursery way.

Nupurasaurus was gentle, patient and sweet,
The best dinosaur you ever could meet.

When five o'clock came, Sammy was a changed boy.
And his parents hearts were filled with joy.

See you tomorrow Sammy!

At Little Darling Childcare, we deliver *"Your Child's Magical Care"*

Magical because it's:

Motivational

Adventurous

Generous

Inspirational

Compassionate

Attentive

Loving

Printed in the United States
By Bookmasters